The **USS ARCHERFISH** *SS311 leaving Hunters Point Naval Shipyard, California, after her last war time overhaul. This* **BALAO** *class submarine is a typical looking late war "Fleet Boat". Install-ed are two 5"/25 cal deck guns, a 40mm single gun mounted on her forward gun deck and a 20mm gun on the after deck. The 20mm gun (less base) was stored in pressure proof lockers adjacent to*

the base mount. Her number 2 periscope is in full raised position. Also raised is the "SD" radar antenna mast. By the arrangement of the limber holes along the lower portion of the superstruc-ture, this boat was built with the Portsmouth plans. The plans between Portsmouth and Electric Boat are slightly different. This photograph was taken June 5, 1945 off Hunters Point. 19N87174

FLEET SUBMARINES
OF WORLD WAR TWO
by Thomas F. Walkowiak

INTRODUCTION

The GATO class, like the later BALAO and TENCH class, were developed from improved versions of the early "T" (SS198-211) class. Orders were plac-ed in 1940 for the FY 1941 shipbuilding program. The design of this subma-rine was frozen so the shipyards could mass produce these boats. The Electric Boat Company of Groton (New London), CT, received the first order for SS212-214. Portsmouth Naval Shipyard in New Hampshire was about to re-ceive an order for three boats (SS218-217), when the Navy went into a major Fleet expansion program. This expansion called for 22 more boats to be built, and Mare Island Naval Shipyard received four of these boats. Eight went to Portsmouth and the balance to EB. Before the ink dried on the contracts, forty-three more boats were ordered. The 1941-42 building called for two more boats (SS283-284) of the GATO design. These two boats went to Mare

Island. A fourth yard, Manitowoc, WI, received orders to build SS265-274. The first submarine to be completed and commissioned was the USS DRUM SS228 built by Portsmouth.

As designed, the early boats had their periscope housing enclosed with a high sail area and bridge. During the war to reduce the silhouette, the super-structure was cut down in stages. As new boats were being built, the latest changes were made to them while building. Although the boats built at EB and Portsmouth were of the same class, external changes can be seen. The most conspicuous was the design of the holes cut into the side of the superstructure to flood and drain it during surfacing and diving. The as built EB boats had a long thin opening above the pressure hull top, while the Portsmouth built boats had an arrangement of limber holes continued aft along the length of the

The **USS RATON** SS270 on sea trials in Lake Michigan after being completed at Manitowoc, Wisconsin Shipyard. This photograph was taken on 1 July 1943. This **GATO** class submarine was equipped with a 4"/50 cal deck gun forward which was the standard submarine gun at the time. This was soon replaced by the specially designed 5"/25 wet mount. Also, mounted at this time is a single 20mm gun on both forward and after gun decks.

NH68814

This close-up of the starboard side of the bridge superstructure of the **USS GATO** SS212 shows the arrangement of the guns, periscopes and other deck gear. This photograph was taken during the boat's overhaul at Mare Island Shipyard in November 1944. The circles indicate new items added during this overhaul. The boat mounts a 4" gun forward and a 20mm gun aft. On the gun deck forward is another 20mm gun and a 40mm gun aft. Note the camouflage countershading under the gun deck extension and the inside of the bridge area. The telephone mounted to a board hanging on the railing was a temporary inport connection.

19N75565

superstructure. The Manitowoc yard built the boats using the EB plans, while Mare Island used the Government plans of its sister yard Portsmouth.

Early in the war, it was discovered that the Japanese depth charges had a maximum explosion depth of 295 feet. The maximum depth of the GATO class submarines was 300 feet. With the ordering of the BALAO class, the hulls were made of HTS (high tensil steel) and thicker than the mild steel hulls of the 212 class. This gave it an operating depth of 400 feet. This class was assigned hull numbers from SS285 through 416, however, when the orders were placed, Manitowoc could not produce this new hull due to production difficulties. The yard didn't make the change over until SS365. It built SS361 to 364 using hull plans for the 212 class, but SS365 through SS378 were of the HTS hulls.

Only 122 boats of the BALAO class were built, with the rest being cancelled. A new yard, Cramps Shipyard of Philadelphia was assigned to build boats of this new class. This yard was assigned boats SS292 through SS303. However, during building, the yard ran into problems and several boats had to be completed by other yards. Cramps used the Portsmouth plans. The first boat completed of this class was the class boat BALAO. Built by Portsmouth, this boat was commissioned on 4 February 1943. Both of these classes took about eight months to build. The USS SEA POACHER SS406 was built in 173 days. During the war, Portsmouth was assigned 108 fleet submarines to build, however, only 80 were completed.

In 1943, when plans were being made to order more boats to be built of the BALAO class, many changes were made and improvements in the design resulted in the TENCH class (SS417-SS525). This class had the BALAO appearance, but the hull design below the water was slightly different and it had a slight increase in the amount of torpedos the boat could carry. Late in the war, when contracts were being cancelled, a large number of this design was struck. Only 31 boats of the class were built. These boats had all the latest equipment installed while being built. However, only a few of these boats saw action during the war. The first boat completed was the USS TENCH SS 417, which was built by Portsmouth.

A total of 52 US Submarines were lost during the war due to enemy action or unknown operational causes. Of these, 27 were of the GATO, BALAO and TENCH classes.

*The recently commissioned **USS BALAO SS285** heads out for sea trials in May 1943. The boat is painted in overall black paint, which was the standard measure of camouflage used at this time. The boat is equipped with a 4"/50 cal gun forward and a 20mm gun on the bridge deck. Due to lack of teak wood for the deck and faster building times this boat like others had only the main walking areas covered in wood. The rest of the main deck was covered with thin perforated metal deck. Like other Portsmouth built boats the anchor is on the port side.* 19N46319

MACHINE GUNS: As designed, the early GATO class submarines had installed a .50 cal machine gun mounted on the after superstructure deck. A pressure and waterproof locker was provided nearby for stowage of the gun and ammunition when submerged. On some boats, a 50 was mounted on the gun foundation on the main deck. Later in the war, the boats carried a portable mounted gun that could be installed on stanchions alongside the sail on the main deck. Some boats carried mountings on the railings near the 40mm guns. Also, .30 cal machine guns were carried in exchange for the 50s. The early guns were water cooled. The later 30s and 50s were all air cooled mounts.

20mm GUN: In 1942, as the 20mm gun became available, this replaced the .50 cal gun as the main anti-aircraft weapon. The gun was mounted in different positions on the boats. Like the .50 cal gun, the weapon was stored in a locker located nearby, only the pedestal base remained. The heavy based MK5 20mm gun was the first one installed, then replaced in November 1944 by the lightweight open MK10 mount. These guns fired at a rate of 450 rounds per minute through a 50 round magazine.

A front view of the forward 40mm gun aboard an unknown submarine. These guns proved to be very effective against small surface targets and aircraft. Some boats had these guns mounted either forward and/or aft on the bridge gun deck. Detail of the shears of this **BALAO** class boat shows the arrangement of the lookout platforms and the range light and PPI antenna. Both scopes are lowered.

USN434018

This early **GATO** class submarine returns to Pearl Harbor after a war patrol. Mounted on the forward deck is a waterjacketed .50 cal machine gun. This gun was soon done away with for the main anti-aircraft weapon. This was replaced by the 20mm gun as this weapon became available to submarines. Note the wearing of the black camouflage paint on the bridge and superstructure. This photograph was taken in 1942.

80G37035

40mm GUN: Late in 1944, the boats started to mount the single 40mm gun. These gave the subs a good medium weapon against aircraft or small boats. The mount was usually carried in the forward and/or after bridge deck locations. This replaced the 20mm gun in most boats. However, a mixed combination of 20s and 40s in different locations can be found on the boats. This gun fired at the rate of 160 RPM.

3"/50 cal gun: As built, the GATOs received a wet 3"/50 cal deck gun. This gun was mounted on the forward gun base on most boats. Soon it was shown that this gun was unsuited, due to its light hitting power. It was soon replaced by the harder hitting 4 inch wet gun.

This top view of the 4"/50 cal deck gun mounted onboard the USS GATO SS212 during her November 1944 overhaul. Note the deck hatches for the stowage of the small boats carried below the main deck. To the left of the gun at the tip of the barrel is the forward marker buoy. The forward escape trunk top hatch is open. To the right of the marker buoy is the access to the escape trunk size door. 19N75563

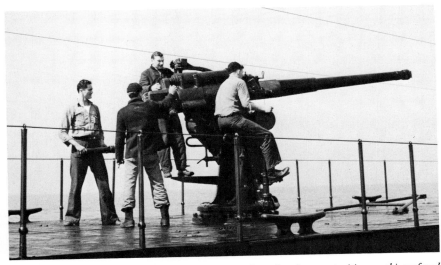

Crewmembers prepare to fire this 3"/50 cal deck gun from the after gun position on this surfaced unknown submarine. This gun was installed as the standard deck gun on all early (1941-43) boats. However, this gun proved to be ineffective and was soon replaced by the 4"/50 cal gun. USN

4"/50 cal GUN: Replacing the 3 inch gun late in 1942, this soon proved inadequate in combat also. This gun was mounted mostly forward on the boats. However, some boats carried it aft while others carried two 4 inch guns. This gun was a stop gap between the lighter 3 inch and the 5 inch gun which replaced the 4 inch.

5"/51 cal GUN: Late in 1943, several boats had a wet 5"/51 cal gun installed. However, only a few had them as a stop gap until the 5"/25 gun came into use. The boats equipped with these guns had an enlarged deck sponson for the working circle of the gun.

5"/25 cal GUN: Work began in 1942 on a wet submarine deck gun. What turned out was a first class weapon that fitted very well into the submarine's role. The production model of this gun started to be delivered to the boats early in 1944, and became the standard deck gun for the Fleet Boats. As the boats entered the shipyards for overhaul, the new guns were added.

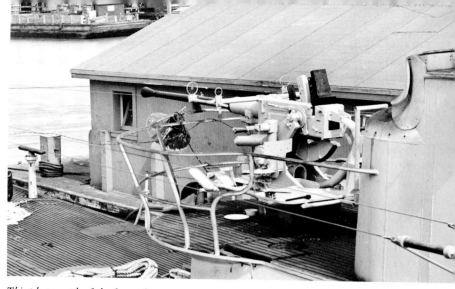

*This photograph of the forward mounted 40mm gun onboard the **USS RATON SS270** was taken in March 1945. The boat just finished an overhaul at Mare Island and is getting ready to start out on another war patrol. The small hatch to the left of the gun on the deck was for ammunition passing.*
80G80436

This photograph of loading a torpedo shows a good view of the 5"/25 cal deck gun. This gun was designed to replace the 4" gun and started to be installed on the fleet boats in 1944. This became the standard gun for all boats to carry. However, some boats went to the end of the war with their 4" guns. Note the salvage air connection on the deck forward of the gun. These were used to salvage a sunken submarine. The number of bolt heads along the side of the plate told the diver which compartment he was at.
USN4265665

*Looking forward from the bridge of the **USS BLUEFISH SS222** while at sea in 1944 shows the forward part of the main deck with a 4" gun and the 20mm gun in the bridge gun deck. This boat was built with only one small boat stowage locker.*
USN

TORPEDOS: Torpedos are the main reason for the submarine and during the early part of the war, the US Navy had bad ones. A lot has been written about this over the years in many books. The Fleet Boat had 6 torpedo tubes forward and 4 aft. The GATOs and BALAOs carried 24 torpedos while the TENCH class carried 28 "fish". By 1944, the torpedo became effective and the sinkings started to mount. Three basic torpedos were used by the Fleet Boats during the war, the MKs 10, 14 and 18, with the MK14 being the most common. This was a steam turbine type with a speed of 31.5 knots at low speed and 46 knots at top speed. The range was 4,500 and 9,000 yards. The warhead was packed with 600 pounds of torpex (TNT). Each fully ready torpedo weighed about 3,000 pounds.

RADARS: "SD" The "SD" radar was the first air warning radar used on submarines. It was developed in 1941 and was installed on all early GATO class boats. This radar had a range of about 20 miles. This radar was replaced late in the war with the "SV" radar.

"SJ" was a surface search radar that appeared in the boats in June 1942. This had a range of about 10 miles. This was replaced by the "SS" radar, however, this didn't appear in the fleet until after the war.

"SV" radar was developed late in the war and was installed on the boats after January 1945.

"SPR-1 & LOOP ANTENNA: The SPR-1 was used for countermeasures and the loop for receiving radio signals at periscope depths.

This close-up view of the **USS MINGO SS261** *shows the newly added "SV" antenna to replace the "SD" and the latest mod of the "SJ" radar. Also added in this July 1945 overhaul are the two 40mm guns added to the gun decks and 5"25 gun aft. A twin 20mm gun is installed on the forward gun base. The gun itself is installed in the pressure proof ready lockers mounted in the bridge superstructure.*
19N87825

This close-up of the **USS GROUPER SS214** *shows the standard arrangement of the "SJ" radar. The radar was mounted forward of the periscopes. The "SD" radar is visible aft of the after lookout platform above the searchlight. The forward torpedo loading hatch is open, ready to loaf "fish". Note the newly added 20mm gun pedestal base.*
19N57195

*Looking aft along the port side of the **USS COD** in February 1945 during overhaul shows the latest additions. A newly designed venturi and gun platform to accommodate the working area for the crew of the new 40mm gun. Both periscopes are raised along with the "SD" mast. The "SJ" radar is located just aft of the scopes.*

19N80100

PERISCOPES: The fleet boats were equipped with two periscopes. These were used for observation and firing of the torpedos. In late 1944, a small radar (ST) was developed to fit in the head of one of the scopes for better ranging of the target.

HYDROPHONE "JP": Mounted on the main deck over the forward torpedo room, this was a passive listening type which was controlled from below.

SONAR (FM): Located on the bottom of the hull forward, this was an active type of sonar.

*The **USS HOE SS258** at Mare Island, in June 1945 has just finished her overhaul and sports a new outfit. Her "SD" has been replaced with the new "SV" antenna and a new hydrophone has been installed.*

19N85964

*Newly added equipment on the **USS COD SS224** in February 1945, is standard refit for all fleet boats. A new tower mast housing for the "SD" mast and a new Torpedo Director Transmitter mounted aft of the "SD" mast for surface firing of torpedeos. All gun platforms have been extended for more working room. This boat has metal decks aft.*

19N80102

right angles at the top. Atop the pressure hull was the raised deck. This deck was several feet above the pressure hull and was covered with wood slats. The 2 1/2″ slats had a 3/4″ gap between them to allow water to flood the area below. The lower sides of the superstructure were either kept clear of the pressure hull or pierced with numerous free flooding openings or limber holes. Above the conning tower which protruded above the wood (main) deck, a free flooding fairwater of light steel plating and framework was built up from the pressure hull. In the fairwater were the bridge, periscope shears and gun platforms.

Early GATOs had a high fairwater as designed and built, however, this was cut down during the war to reduce the boats silhouette. The housing or shears for the periscopes on the BALAO and TENCH classes were built with a heavy housing for better support to the periscopes, whereas the GATOs had a thin support housing. Also, mounted on the bridge was a target bearing transmitter used for torpedo surface attack.

*Close-up detail of the shears of the **USS POGY SS266** in August 1944. This photograph shows the arrangement of the "SJ" radar forward of the scopes which was the practice with the GATO's at this time. When the new "SD" mast housing was installed aft of the shears, the "SJ" was moved to where the "SD" is now.*   19N80888

HULL STRUCTURE: The inner or pressure hull was made out of 9/6″ mild steel for the GATOs and 7/8″ HTS steel for the BALAOs and TENCH classes. This pressure hull was 16″ in diameter and was 174 feet long. The conning tower sat atop the pressure hull. This hull was divided into 8 compartments: forward torpedo room, forward battery, control room, after battery, forward engine room, after engine room, maneuvering room and after torpedo room. Between the pressure hull and the outer hull are the fuel and ballast tanks. These tanks were not pressure proof and had a water compensation system to equalize the pressure.

The outer hull was generally of light all-welded construction. However, some of the tanks inside the outer hull were made of the same steel as the pressure hull, due to these tanks being able to withstand the submerged pressure. The upper end of the outer hull curved over to join the pressure hull at

A section of a submarine loaded on the crawler at the Manitowac Shipyard. This prefab technique speeded up the building time of the boats and some boats were built in 9 months.   NH68806

The **USS HAMMERHEAD** SS364 *slides sideways into the water during her launching at Manitowac Shipyards on October 24, 1943. Note the detail of the bilge keel. This yard used the plans supplied by Electric Boat.* N70972

This view shows several boats being built on the shipways at Cramp Shipyard in Philadelphia in July 1945. The boat on the left still has not received the superstructure main deck or bridge. The boat to the right is just about complete. 19N85907

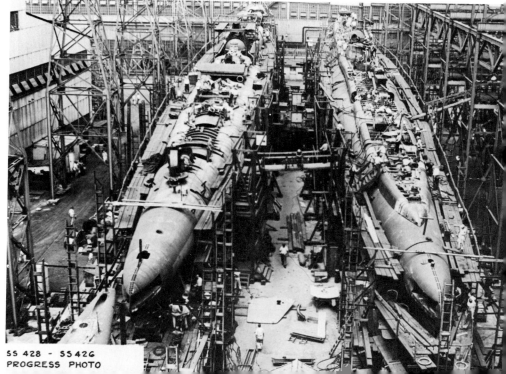

SS 428 - SS 426
PROGRESS PHOTO

PROPULSION AND CONTROL: The main propulsion plant for the fleet type submarines was a conventional diesel-electric drive. Three different manufacturers provided the diesel engines: General Motors, Fairbanks-Morse and Hooven-Owen-Rentschler. This latter one was replaced by either the GM or F-M types. Four engines were installed in each boat and each engine could produce 1,600 HP which drove the main generators. These generators were 415-volt DC and produced 1,100 kw of power. The power was then used to drive the main motors. The four main motors were rated at 1,375 HP each. Two motors were used to drive each propeller shaft through a combining and reduction gear.

The diesel engines were used for surface running only. Snorkel installations were not operational during the war. While submerged, the main motors were powered by two sets of storage batteries. Each set contained 126 cells. Each cell weighed 1,650 pounds and was 21x15 inches by 54 inches high. The batteries were charged by the diesel engines while surfaced.

The folding bow planes controlled the depth, up or down, without change in the angle of the boat. The angle of the boat was controlled by the stern planes. These planes required the boat to be moving to operate. On the surface, the bow planes folded up against the superstructure. The stern planes being below the waterline while surfaced were fixed. Steering was controlled by a single hydraulic powered rudder mounted on the centerline.

*This drydock view of the stern of the **USS RASHER SS269** was taken in December 1944. The detail of the stern planes and propeller are clear however, the rudder which is located on the center line is in shadow.*
19N72604

*Looking at the starboard side of the **USS SKATE SS305** during completion at Mare Island in July 1943. Her bow planes are rigged in the down position and the Flooding/drain holes and ladder cutouts are seen in the superstructure. This is hidden when the planes are in the up position. Mare Island, being a government shipyard used the Portsmouth plans for building. Note the arrangement of the holes and the anchor is on the port side.*
19N49902

11

Wearing overall Black paint the **USS KINGFISH SS234** *is seen here in the June 7, 1943 photo. At this time, the standard practice was to paint the boats in this measure.*
USN

CAMOUFLAGE

When the first of the GATOs started to appear in the fleet, they were painted in overall black. This measure was tested and found to be the overall best camouflage for submerged submarines. The instructions appeared in the release of "Ship's Two", which was the term used for the instructions for ships camouflage. This edition was released in January 1941. This instruction called for the entire submarine to be painted black above the waterline. It called for the painting of the capstans, running boards, rails and all parts visible from the air. The underbody was to have a black anti-fouling paint type applied.

Early in the war, experiments were carried out in Pearl Harbor on a very dark blue paint, which was found to be even less visible than black for submerged submarines in the Hawaiian waters. However, this dark blue paint deteriorated and turned milky in a few weeks, whereas the black paint remained serviceable for several months. It was noted that "improved formulas of Pearl Harbor blue are being tested extensively in the Fleet at present." However, it is very hard to determine which boats had this blue paint applied. The reason is that most photos are in black and white. A faded black could be mistaken for a fresh dark blue paint. No list has ever come to light to list which boats had this paint and when. Nor, could a color chip of this paint be found.

In June 1944, two new special submarine measures were released to the fleet. Both used extensive spray techniques to countershade and flatten the boat, blending it into the background. These colors were of neutral gray shades. Painting drawings were produced for the two basic camouflage designs. The designs called for several shades of gray blending into each other. Measure 32/3SS-B popularly known as the "light gray job" was very effective during surface operations, at night and on overcast days. The other was known as the "dark gray job", Measure 32/9SS. This was the same basic pattern but with a darker level of grays.

These instructions seem to be followed until the end of the war. Some boats retained their black paint until the war's end. Slight variations can be seen in photographs of submarines during this time period.

The **USS FLYING FISH SS229** leaving Hunters Point Naval Shipyard, for testing of her newly added mine detection and clearance equipment. In May she would make her twelfth and last war patrol wearing this measure 32 camouflage paint scheme. The boat is equipped with a 20mm gun forward and a 40mm gun aft. A 5"/25 cal. gun is mounted on the main deck aft.   USN

A drydock photograph of the **USS POMPON SS267** with a fresh coat of the new 32/3SS-B camouflage paint scheme. The forward part of the superstructure and the bridge is painted with Haze Gray and the after part is #16 Medium Gray which blends into black aft.   19N75576

13

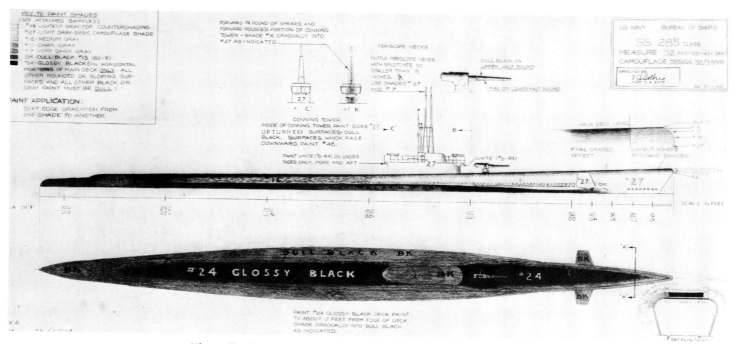

These official camouflage design drawings were drawn up in June of 1944. They were approved by the camouflage branch chief Mr. Everett Warner and a Bureau of Ships Navy captain. These paints were all natural grays.

USN

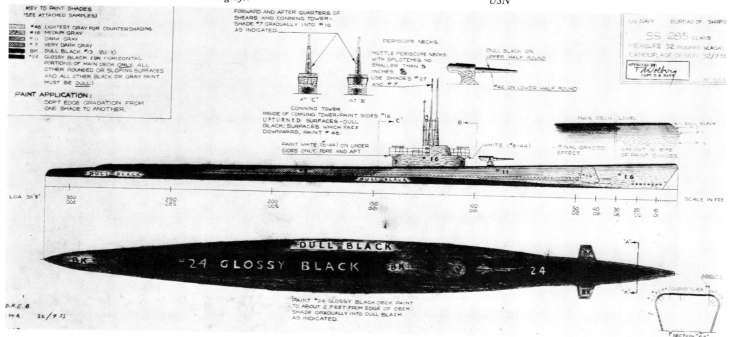

USS GATO SS212
Sept. 1943

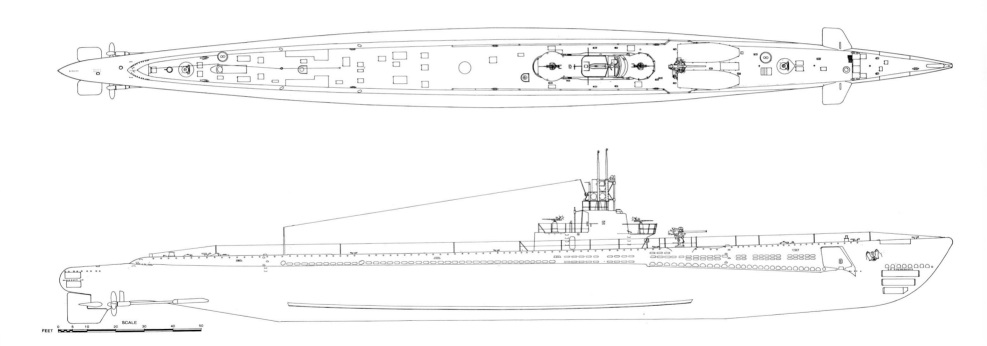

SCALE

FEET 0 5 10   20   30   40   50

*The **USS GRUNION** SS216 upon completion at Electric Boat Company in March 1942. This configuration with the enclosed shears was as designed. Soon this was cut away to lessen the surface silhouette. This was done in stages during the course of the war. The **GRUNION** was lost in July 1942 and probably looked like this at the time of her sinking.*

USN

GATO Class
SS212-284
GENERAL INFORMATION

Length Overall	311'-9"
Extreme Beam	27'-3"
Standard Displacement	1,526 tons
Submerged Displacement	2,424 tons
Designed Complement	6 Officers-54 Men(1)
Designed Depth	300 feet
Designed Speed:Surface	20.25 knts.
Submerged	8.75 knts.
Engines:Diesel	5,400 SHP
Fuel:	97,140 gals.

(1) Standard crew 85 (WW2).

ARMAMENT
Main:10 Torpedo Tubes
Torpedoes:24
Secondary:1-3"/50 cal (1941-43)
    1-4"/50 cal (1943-45)
    1 or 2-5"/25 cal (1944-45)
Anti-Aircraft:1 or 2-40mm single (1944-45)
    1 or 2-20mm single (1942-45)
    2-.50 cal MG (1941-45)
    2-.30 cal MG (1942-45)

A total of 73 GATO class submarines were built during 1941-45. Of these 19 were sunk during the war. These boats, along with the BALAO and TENCH class that were also built during the war, became the standard FLEET BOAT of WW2. The USS DRUM SS228 was the first boat to be commissioned and was built by Portsmouth Naval Yard, NH, on 1 November 1941. These boats were also known as the "thin-skinned boats" due to having a thinner pressure hull than the later BALAO or TENCH classes.

These boats were developed through the design process of the preceding classes that followed before. The eight compartments and conning towers were all designed so if any one or even two were flooded the boat would be sealed off from these flooded compartments. Also, the boat would be able to surface. The GATOs had two escape hatches that were located in both of the torpedo rooms, which enabled a diving bell to hook up for the rescue of the crew in a shallow sunken boat. Also, it was possible to make a free ascent escape from any other compartment that had a hatch. All boats had deck fitting where salvage air could be blown into the compartment from a rescue ship to raise the boat.

The early GATOs, as built, had two small boats stowed below the forward part of the superstructure, however, the later boats only had one. Each boat had a rescue buoy mounted both fore and aft in the superstructure deck. These buoys can be released from inside the boat and are attached by cable to the sub. The buoy has a message stating that a submarine is sunk here. This is a standard item and can be found on all subs.

4755-42 U.S.S. WAHOO (SS-238)
PLAN VIEW AFT.
MARE ISLAND, CAL. 8/10/42.

4755-42 U.S.S. WAHOO (SS238)
PLAN VIEW AFT.
MARE ISLAND, CAL. AUGUST 10, 1942

The **USS WAHOO SS238** at Mare Island in August 1942. The first step in cutting down the silhouette by the removal of the after portion of the fairwater. A "SJ" radar mast has been installed to the forward of the scopes which was standard practice at this time for the **GATO** class boats. USN

The GATOs can easily be distinguished from the later boats by the thin tube-like periscope housing. Also, the boats can be distinguished as to what yard built them by the arrangement of the anchors or limber holes along the superstructure.

Hull	Name	Builder	Comm	Decom	Fate
SS212	GATO	EB	12/31/41	03/01/60	Scrapped 7/60
SS213	GEENLING	''	01/21/42	03/01/60	Scrapped 7/60
SS214	GROUPER	''	02/12/42	12/02/68	Scrapped 8/70
SS215	GROWLER	''	03/20/42		Sunk 11/08/44
SS216	GRUNION	''	04/11/42		Lost 07/30/42
SS217	GUARDFISH	''	05/08/42	06/01/60	Target 10/61
SS218	ALBACORE	''	06/01/42		Sunk 11/07/44
SS219	AMBERJACK	''	06/19/42		Sunk 02/16/43
SS220	BARB	''	07/08/42	02/05/54	Italy 12/54
					Scrapped 10/72

Heading out for sea-trials in October 1942, the **USS RUNNER SS275,** will soon make her first war patrol in early 1943. This Portsmouth built boat had the anchor mounted on the port side and a high bridge as built. This would soon be cut down. Her "SJ" radar is mounted in front of her number one scope.
USN

17

SS221	BLACKFISH	"	07/22/42	05/19/54	Scrapped 5/59
SS222	BLUEFISH	"	05/24/43	11/20/53	Scrapped 6/60
SS223	BONEFISH	"	05/31/43		Sunk 06/18/45
SS224	COD	"	06/21/43	06/30/71	Museum-Cleveland, OH

SS225	CERO	"	07/04/43	12/01/62	Scrapped 9/70
SS226	CORVINA	"	08/06/43		Sunk 11/16/43
SS227	DARTER	"	9/07/43		Grounded 10/24/44
SS228	DRUM	Ports	11/01/41	12/01/62	Museum-Mobile, AL

The **USS AMBERJACK SS219** is shown here leaving the Electric Boat Company building yards in May 1942. The early built boats were completed with the enclosed scope supports and high bridge (Fairwater). The boat mounts a 3"/50 cal. gun aft and like most early boats has mine cable cutting devices mounted forward in a retractable opening in the hull. The boat was lost in February 1943 while on a war patrol. USN

The **USS SNOOK SS279** is shown here in this January 11, 1943 photograph taken during sea trials. This boat shows the next step of removal of the fairwater. The metal around the scopes and the front part of the fairwater have been removed. A 20mm gun both fore and aft have been added. However, this gun had the heavy cast base which was soon replaced with the tripod type base. 19N39696

SS229	FLYING FISH	''	12/10/41	05/28/54	Scrapped 5/59
SS230	FINBACK	''	01/31/42	04/21/50	Scrapped 7/59
SS231	HADDOCK	''	03/14/42		Scrapped 8/60
SS232	HALIBUT	''	04/10/42	07/18/45	Scrapped 12/46
SS233	HERRING	''	05/04/42		Sunk 6/44
SS234	KINGFISH	''	05/20/42	03/01/60	Scrapped 11/60
SS235	SHAD	''	06/12/42	04/01/42	Scrapped 7/60
SS236	SILVERSIDES	MI	12/15/41	06/30/69	Museum Muskegon, MI
SS237	TRIGGER	''	01/31/42		Sunk 03/28/45
SS238	WAHOO	''	05/15/42		Sunk 10/11/42

By now, the length of the fairwater was reduced and by 1944 this was the basic shape of the fairwater. This view of the **USS MINGO SS261** *which is painted in overall black, was taken in February 1944 during refit at Mare Island. Tripod legs have replaced the cast bases for the 20mm guns and the 4"/50 cal. deck gun has been installed. The paint looks glossy but this is due to the rain.*
19N62321

A close up of the fairwater looking aft along the starboard side of the **USS TRIGGER SS237.** *This photograph was taken in August 1944 during refit at Mare Island. The black circles show new items installed during this refit which include a new ''SJ'' radar, venturi, 4"/50 cal. deck gun and searchlight.*
19N83829

The **USS BLUEFISH SS222** *during sea-trials in 1943. This boat was built by E. B. and was commissioned with the cut down fairwater. It also had a 20mm gun mounted on the forward gun platform. The "SJ" radar is mounted in front of the scopes as was the practice at this time period.*   USN

Looking up at the aft part of the lookout platform of the **USS BLUEFISH SS222** *during sea-trials. Most boats mounted a 9" signal searchlight aft of the shears on a swinging arm bracket. The "SD" antenna can be seen behind the light and on top of the lookout platform pipe rail are fittings mounted to mount a machine gun into.*   USN

This close-up of the bridge of the **USS TRIGGER SS237** *was taken in August 1944 during refit. Details of the compass repeater, target bearing transmitter and alarm switches are seen behind the protective venturi shield. The hatch leading to the conning tower is at right on the deck. The pole in the center of the photograph is the mast for the "SJ" antenna. This shot was taken from the port lookout platform. The* **TRIGGER** *was lost in March 1945.*   19N83827

SS239	WHALE	,,	06/01/42		60 Scrapped 10/60
SS240	ANGLER	EB	10/01/43	12/15/71	Scrapped 1970s
SS241	BASHAW	,,	10/25/43	09/13/69	Scrapped 7/72
SS242	BLUEGILL	,,	11/11/43	06/28/69	Scrapped 12/70
SS243	BREAM	,,	01/24/44	06/28/69	Scrapped 11/69
SS244	CAVALLA	,,	03/29/44	12/30/69	Museum Galveston, TX
SS245	COBIA	,,	03/29/44	07/01/70	Museum Manitowoc, WI
SS246	CROAKER	,,	04/21/44	12/20/71	Museum Groton, CT
					Repossess 1987
SS247	DACE	,,	07/23/43	01/15/54	Italy 55, Scrapped 75
SS248	DORADO	,,	08/28/44		Sunk 10/12/43
SS249	FLASHER	,,	9/25/43	03/16/46	Scrapped 6/63
SS250	FLIER	,,	10/18/43		Sunk 08/13/44

SS251	FLOUNDER	,,	11/29/43	02/12/47	Scrapped 2/60
SS252	GABILAN	,,	12/28/43	02/23/46	Scrapped 1/60
SS253	GUNNEL	,,	08/20/42	05/18/46	Scrapped 12/59
SS254	GURNARD	,,	09/18/42	06/ /60	Scrapped 10/61
SS255	HADDO	,,	10/09/42	02/16/46	Scrapped 5/59
SS256	HAKE	,,	10/30/42	04/19/68	Scrapped 12/72
SS257	HARDER	,,	12/02/42		Sunk 08/24/44
SS258	HOE	,,	12/16/42	04/15/60	Scrapped 9/60
SS259	JACK	,,	01/06/43	04/21/58	Greece 4/58 Target 9/67
SS260	LAPON	,,	1/23/43	08/10/57	Scrapped 1979
SS261	MINGO	,,	02/12/43	08/15/55	Japan 8/55 Scrapped 11/71
SS262	MUSKALLUNGE	,,	03/15/43	01/18/57	Brazil 1/57
					Target 7/68

The after portion of the MINGO, during the February 1944 refit. The after torpedo loading hatch is open along with some access hatches in the main deck. Details can be seen of the after escape hatch and marker buoy. This EB designed boat has a full length wood deck.　19N62322

SS263	PADDLE	"	03/29/43	01/18/57	Brazil 1/57Scrapped 1/69
SS264	PARGO	"	04/26/43	12/01/60	Scrapped 5/61
SS265	PETO	Man	11/21/42	08/01/60	Scrapped 11/60
SS266	POGY	"	01/10/43	07/20/46	Scrapped 5/59
SS267	POMPON	"	03/17/43	04/01/60	Scrapped 12/60
SS268	PUFFER	"	04/27/43	06/10/60	Scrapped 12/60
SS269	RASHER	"	06/08/43	12/20/71	Scrapped 8/74
SS270	RATON	"	07/13/43	06/28/69	Scrapped 10/73
SS271	RAY	"	07/27/43	09/30/58	Scrapped 12/60
SS272	REDFIN	"	08/31/43	07/01/70	Scrapped 3/71
SS273	ROBALO	"	09/28/43		Sunk 7/26/44
SS274	ROCK	"	10/26/43	09/13/69	Scrapped 8/72
SS275	RUNNER	Ports	07/30/42		Missing 6/43
SS276	SAWFISH	"	08/26/42	04/01/60	Scrapped 12/60
SS277	SCAMP	"	09/18/42		Sunk 11/16/44
SS278	SCORPION	"	10/01/42		Sunk 01/05/44
SS279	SNOOK	"	10/24/42		Sunk 04/08/45
SS280	STEELHEAD	"	12/07/42	04/01/60	Scrapped 7/61
SS281	SUNFISH	MI	07/15/42	05/01/60	Scrapped 12/60
SS282	TUNNY	"	09/01/42	06/28/69	Scrapped 6/70
SS283	TINOSA	"	01/15/43	12/02/53	Target 11/60
SS284	TULLIBEE	"	02/15/43		Sunk 03/26/44

The USS HARDER SS257 is seen here in this February 1944 photograph taken at Mare Island during refit. The newly installed gun access hatch and door is seen on the forward part of the bridge. Also, a 5"/51 cal gun has been installed with an extension added to the deck. The pressure proof locker is for ready service ammunition. Added to the front of the number 1 scope is a re-inforcing guard to protect the scope housing during crash dives. The "SJ" metal radar mast has been moved to behind the scopes. The 5"/51 gun was only added to a few boats in late 1943 and early 1944. 19N62481

The USS HADDO SS255 leaving for another war patrol after leaving the refit yard in April 1945. This boat has all the latest additions added to the boats at this time. A 5"/25 cal gun aft, 40mm gun forward, "SD" mast housing and a new camouflage paint job. This boat was scrapped in 1959.
19N83115

This EB built boat sports added limber holes along the superstructure to increase the rate water floods and drains. This was done to some of the EB designed boats during the war but not all. Also small holes were cut in the rounding top of the superstructure deck where it meets the main deck to let trapped air escape faster. The bow planes have been tilted for better performance. This was done to all new constructions and as boats entered refit this modification was made to the planes.   19N80123

This October 24, 1942 view of the **USS SUNFISH SS281** was taken at Mare Island during refit. A newly added 20mm gun was mounted aft on the gun deck along with a flare pot. This boat was built by Mare Island using the Portsmouth Government plans. In the background is the **USS BUSHNELL AS15** being built. The submarine tender saw many years of service.   USN

The **USS STEELHEAD** SS280 getting ready to get underway after completing her last war time refit. This photograph was taken on April 10, 1945 at Hunters Point Shipyard. The circles indicate the changes made in this view. Along the top edge of the superstructure are a series of holes between the frames to let trapped air escape during diving.

USN

This close-up of the **USS RASHER** SS269 was taken in December 1944 during refit. Note all the up to date changes made. She had a new "SD" mast installed along with a new periscope on which the tops have been all camouflaged. A new pressure proof ready service locker has been added for the 20mm ammo drums just forward of the 20mm gun. To the far left of this picture the hoist from the after battery compartment can just be seen. This was for passing 5" ammo up to the after gun.

19N79603

BALAO CLASS

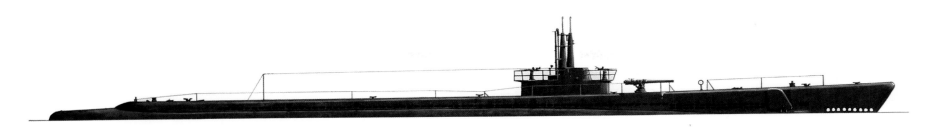

USS BOWFIN SS287 in May 1943 wearing the Ms 9 overall black camouflage.

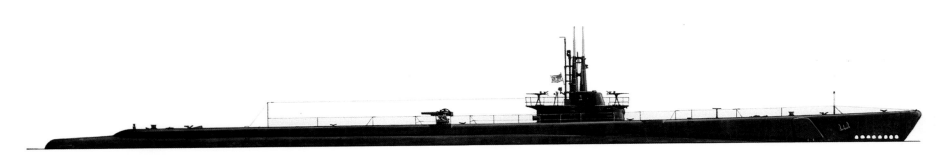

USS ICEFISH SS367 in June 1944 wearing the Ms 9 overall black camouflage.

USS PAMPANITO SS383 in July 1945 wearing Ms 32/3SS-B camouflage
scheme.

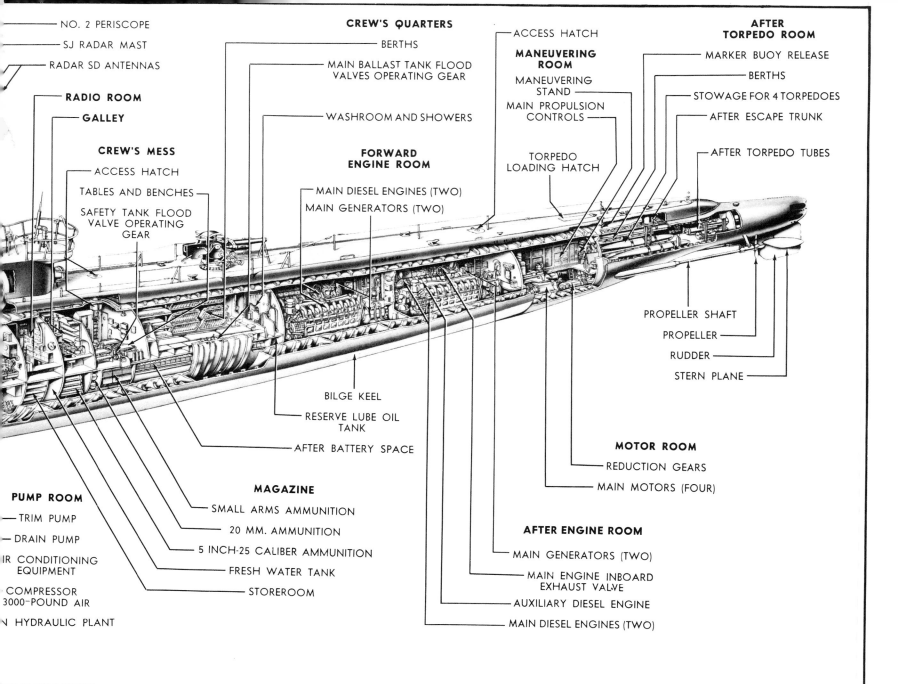

NO. 2 PERISCOPE

SJ RADAR MAST

RADAR SD ANTENNAS

RADIO ROOM

GALLEY

CREW'S MESS

ACCESS HATCH

TABLES AND BENCHES

SAFETY TANK FLOOD
VALVE OPERATING
GEAR

CREW'S QUARTERS

BERTHS

MAIN BALLAST TANK FLOOD
VALVES OPERATING GEAR

WASHROOM AND SHOWERS

**FORWARD
ENGINE ROOM**

MAIN DIESEL ENGINES (TWO)

MAIN GENERATORS (TWO)

ACCESS HATCH

**MANEUVERING
ROOM**

MANEUVERING
STAND

MAIN PROPULSION
CONTROLS

TORPEDO
LOADING HATCH

**AFTER
TORPEDO ROOM**

MARKER BUOY RELEASE

BERTHS

STOWAGE FOR 4 TORPEDOES

AFTER ESCAPE TRUNK

AFTER TORPEDO TUBES

PROPELLER SHAFT

PROPELLER

RUDDER

STERN PLANE

BILGE KEEL

RESERVE LUBE OIL
TANK

AFTER BATTERY SPACE

PUMP ROOM

TRIM PUMP

DRAIN PUMP

IR CONDITIONING
EQUIPMENT

COMPRESSOR
3000-POUND AIR

N HYDRAULIC PLANT

MAGAZINE

SMALL ARMS AMMUNITION

20 MM. AMMUNITION

5 INCH-25 CALIBER AMMUNITION

FRESH WATER TANK

STOREROOM

AFTER ENGINE ROOM

MAIN GENERATORS (TWO)

MAIN ENGINE INBOARD
EXHAUST VALVE

AUXILIARY DIESEL ENGINE

MAIN DIESEL ENGINES (TWO)

MOTOR ROOM

REDUCTION GEARS

MAIN MOTORS (FOUR)

RRANGEMENT

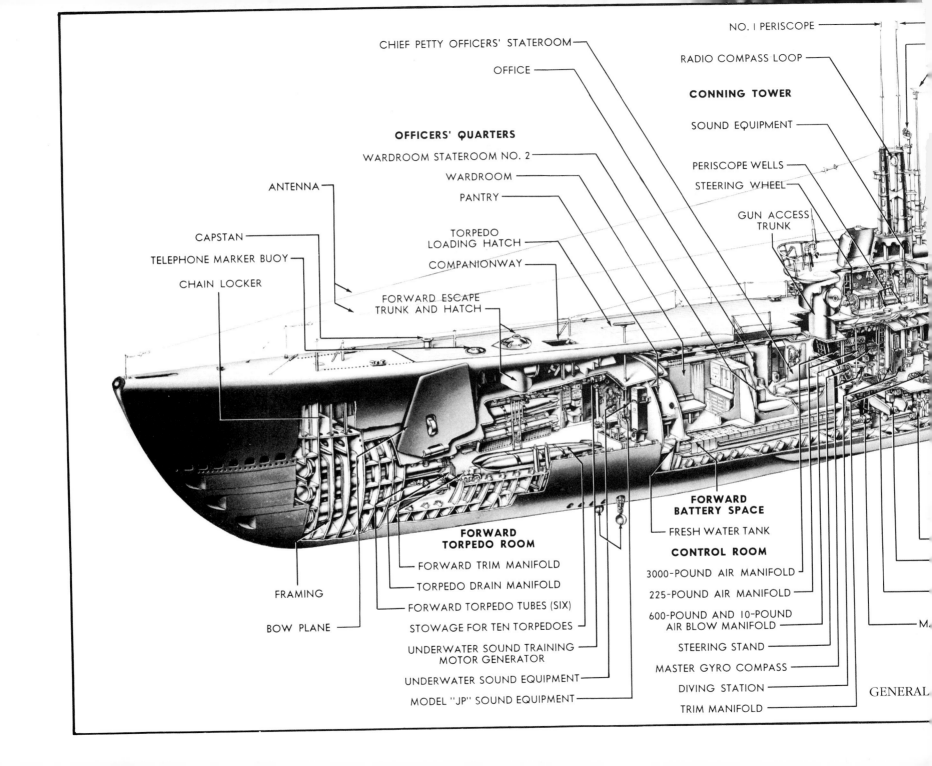

CHIEF PETTY OFFICERS' STATEROOM

OFFICE

NO. I PERISCOPE

RADIO COMPASS LOOP

CONNING TOWER

SOUND EQUIPMENT

OFFICERS' QUARTERS

WARDROOM STATEROOM NO. 2

WARDROOM

PANTRY

PERISCOPE WELLS

STEERING WHEEL

ANTENNA

GUN ACCESS TRUNK

CAPSTAN

TORPEDO LOADING HATCH

TELEPHONE MARKER BUOY

COMPANIONWAY

CHAIN LOCKER

FORWARD ESCAPE TRUNK AND HATCH

FORWARD BATTERY SPACE

FRESH WATER TANK

FORWARD TORPEDO ROOM

CONTROL ROOM

FORWARD TRIM MANIFOLD

3000-POUND AIR MANIFOLD

FRAMING

TORPEDO DRAIN MANIFOLD

225-POUND AIR MANIFOLD

FORWARD TORPEDO TUBES (SIX)

600-POUND AND 10-POUND AIR BLOW MANIFOLD

BOW PLANE

STOWAGE FOR TEN TORPEDOES

STEERING STAND

UNDERWATER SOUND TRAINING MOTOR GENERATOR

MASTER GYRO COMPASS

UNDERWATER SOUND EQUIPMENT

DIVING STATION

GENERAL

MODEL "JP" SOUND EQUIPMENT

TRIM MANIFOLD

TENCH CLASS

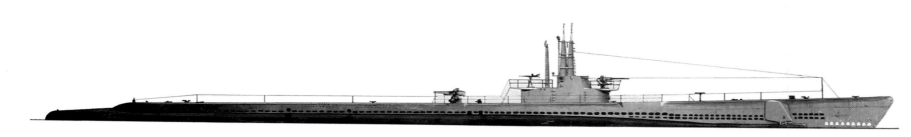

USS THORNBACK SS418 in March 1945 wearing Ms 32/3SS-B camouflage
scheme.

USS TIRANTE SS420 in June 1945 wearing Ms 32/9SS camouflage scheme.

USS RUNNER SS476 in August 1945 wearing Ms 32/9SS camouflage scheme.

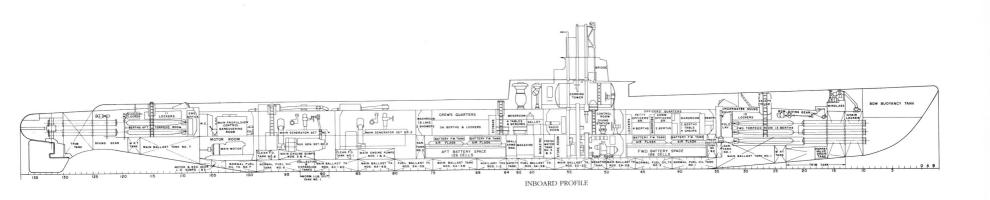

INBOARD PROFILE

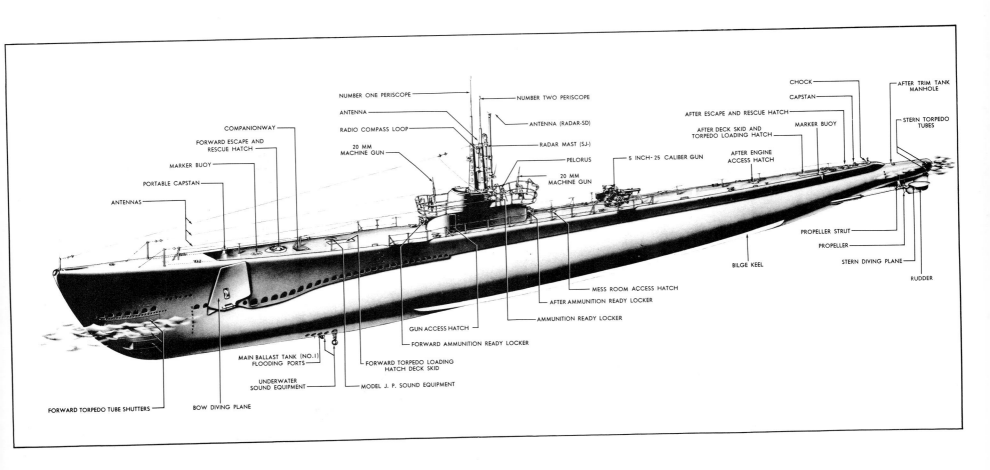

GATO CLASS

USS GATO SS212 in Sept. 1942 wearing Ms 9 overall black camouflage.

USS GROUPER SS214 in July 1945 wearing Ms 32/3SS-B camouflage scheme.

USS WAHOO SS238 in July 1943 wearing the Ms 9 overall black camouflage.

Like alot of GATO's the **USS BREAM SS243** *is seen here in post war service. This photo was taken on 1 January 1962 off the coast of Hawaii. The fairwater has been streamlined and all guns removed. Also, she has been fitted with an enlarged sonar dome on her bow. This boat became a hunter-killer (SSK) boat in 1951. They were used for attacking other submarines.* USN1059531

The former **USS MINGO SS261** *is seen here as the Japanese* **KUROSHIO.** *This boat was turned over to the Japanese in 1955 to serve in the self-defense forces. She rests at buoy at U.S. Fleet Activities, Yokosuka, Japan. Ten years before, this boat was sinking Japanese warships.* USN682257

USS BALAO SS285
Oct. 1944

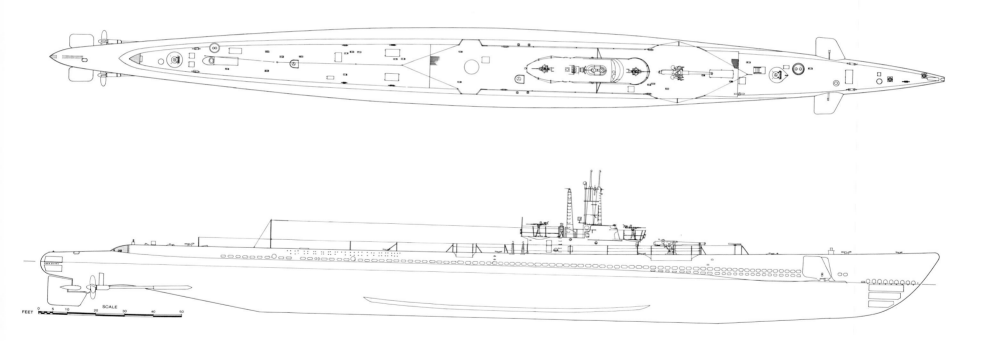

SCALE

FEET   0   5   10   20   30   40   50

*The **USS BALAO SS285** upon completion in May 1943. The boat has just left Portsmouth Shipyard for sea trials. As built, the early **BALAO's** were equipped with the 4" gun and 20mm guns on the gun decks. Soon these would be replaced with the 5"/25's. The boat is painted in overall black, which was the measure in use at this time.*

19N46317

BALAO Class
SS285-SS416
GENERAL INFORMATION

Length Overall	311'-9"	
Extreme Beam	27'4"	
Standard Displacement	1,526 tons	
Submerged Displacement	2,414 tons	
Designed Complement:	6 Officers 60 Men (1)	
Designed Depth:	400 feet	
Designed Speed:Surface	20.25 knts	
Submerged	8.75 knts	
Engines:Diesel	5,400 SHP	
Fuel	94,000-116,000 gals	

(1) Standard crew 85 (WW2)

ARMAMENT
Torpedo Tubes:10
Torpedoes:24
Secondary:1-3"/50 cal (1943)
    1-4"/50 cal (1943-45)
    1 or 2-5"/25 cal (1944-45)
Anti-aircraft:1 or 2-20mm single (1943-45)
    1 or 2-40mm single (1944-45)
    2-.50 cal MG (1943-45)
    2-.30 cal MG (1943-45)

An improved version of the GATO class with a thicker pressure hull, the basic design of the BALAOs is the same. A total of 132 boats were ordered, but SS296 sunk while being built and SS353-360, 379, 380 were cancelled in 1944. The first boat commissioned was the USS BALAO SS285 on 27 October 1942. This boat was built by Portsmouth Navy Yard, NH.

Out of the 121 boats that saw service during the war, 10 were lost. Most of these boats served in the postwar Navy and many were used by foreign navies. Like the GATOs, these boats saw a lot of changes made to them after the war. Most had all their deck guns removed and the superstructure streamlined. These boats were also known as the "thick-skinned boats", due to the almost 1" thick pressure hulls. The best way to distinguish the BALAOs from the GATOs is by the heavy periscope housing.

*This head on view of the **USS CABRILLA SS288** was taken in June 1943 on sea trials. The hole in the bow is called the "bull-nose" and is used for mooring the ship or towing. Like other Portsmouth designed boats, the anchor is on the port side. This boat is equipped with a 4" gun and tripod mounted 20mm gun forward. Like the **GATO's**, alot of these boats only had wood main decks in the gun areas. The bulge in the left side of the bridge is for clearance of the access hatch for the bridge.*

19N48984

*The **USS SKATE SS305** during building at Mare Island in July 1943. During inport periods, the boats were equipped with propeller guards. But, these were removable and were taken off before going on war patrol. The small holes in the after portion of the superstructure and stern are air vents. The **SKATE** was used after the war as a target ship in the atom bomb test at Bikini in July 1946. She was finally sunk in 1948 after tests were complete.*

19N49901

SS285	BALAO	Ports	02/04/43	07/11/63	Target 9/63
SS286	BILLFISH	''	04/20/43	04/01/68	Scrapped 3/71
SS287	BOWFIN	''	05/01/43	12/01/71	Museum Pearl Harbor, HI
SS288	CABRILLA	''	05/24/43	06/30/68	Scrapped 4/72
SS289	CAPELIN	''	06/04/4		Missing 12/43
SS290	CISCO	''	05/10/43		Sunk 09/28/43
SS291	CREVALLE	''	06/24/43	68	Scrapped 3/71
SS292	DEVILFISH	Cramp	09/01/44	60s	Target 8/68
SS293	DRAGONET	''	03/06/44	04/16/46	Scuttled 9/61
SS294	ESCOLAR	''	06/02/44		Sunk 10/17/44
SS295	HACKLEBACK	''	11/07/44	60s	Scrapped 12/68
SS296	LANCETFISH	''/Bos	02/12/45	03/24/45	Incomplete Scrapped 8/59
SS297	LING	''/Bos	06/08/45	12/01/71	Museum Hackensack, NJ
SS298	LIONFISH	''/Ports	11/01/44	12/20/71	Museum Fall River, MA
SS299	MANTA	''/Ports	12/18/44	06/30/67	Target 7/69
SS300	MORAY	''	01/26/45	60s	Target 6/70
SS301	RONCADOR	''	03/27/45	12/01/71	Scrapped 70s
SS302	SABALO	''	06/19/45	07/01/71	Target 71
SS303	SABLEFISH	''	12/18/45	69	Scrapped 7/71
SS304	SEAHORSE	MI	03/31/43	60s	Scrapped 12/68
SS305	SKATE	''	04/15/43	12/11/46	Target 7/46 Bikini
SS306	TANG	''	10/15/43		Sunk 10/24/44
SS307	TILEFISH	''	12/15/43	05/04/60	Venezuela Scrapped 1/77
SS308	APOGON	''	07/16/43		Target 07/25/46 Bikini
SS309	ASPRO	Ports	07/31/43	09/07/62	Target 11/62
SS310	BATFISH	''	08/21/43	11/01/60	Museum Muskogee, OK
SS311	ARCHERFISH	''	09/04/43	05/01/68	Target 10/68
SS312	BURRFISH	''	09/13/43	05/11/61	CANADA Scrapped 70s
SS313	PERCH	EB	01/07/44	12/01/71	Scrapped 71
SS314	SHARK	''	02/14/44		Sunk 10/24/44
SS315	SEALION	''	03/08/44	02/20/70	Scuttled 76
SS316	BARBEL	EB	04/03/44		Target 10/64
SS318	BAYA	''	05/20/44	10/30/72	Scrapped 10/73
SS319	BECUNA	''	5/27/44	06/30/71	Museum Phila.,PA
SS320	BERGALL	''	06/12/44	10/18/58	Turkey Stricken 78
SS321	BESUGO	''	06/19/44	03/31/66	Italy 3/66 Scrapped 4/76
SS322	BLACKFIN	''	07/04/44	09/15/72	Target 70s
SS323	CAIMAN	''	07/17/44	06/30/72	Turkey 6/72
SS324	BLENNY	''	07/27/44	11/07/69	Target 70s
SS325	BLOWER	''	08/10/44	11/16/50	Turkey 11/50
SS326	BLUEBACK	''	08/28/44	05/23/48	Turkey 5/48
SS327	BOARFISH	''	09/23/44	05/23/48	Turkey 5/48 Stricken 78
SS328	CHARR	''	09/23/44	12/20/71	Scrapped 8/72
SS329	CHUB	''	10/21/44	05/23/48	Turkey 5/48 Scrapped 78

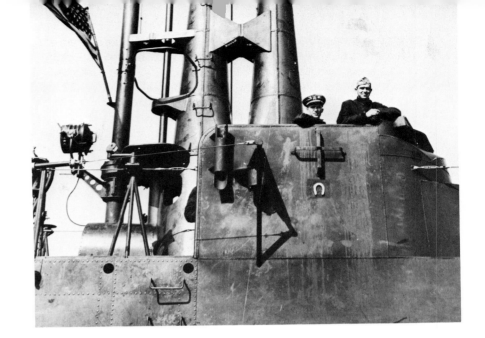

*The **USS HARDHEAD** SS365 during training cruise in the Great Lakes in April 1944. This boat was built by the Manitowoc Shipbuilding Co., Manitowoc, Wisconsin. After the brief training cruise the boats were put into a floating drydock and towed down the Mississippi to New Orleans. The Manitowoc yard built boats using the plans prepared by Electric Boat Co. The cross above the ships ''Lucky Horseshoe'' is for the stowage of the life ring.* NH70963, 70976

A good stern view of the prop and rudder area. The stern planes are being held in position by temporary supports during this construction photograph taken at Cramp Shipbuilding in April 1943. Still to be fitted is metal around the torpedo tubes and the lower outer door.   19N43763

A standard looking ''Fleet Boat'' of 1944. This is the **USS TILEFISH SS307** on sea trials after being completed at Mare Island in April. Painted in black, she carries a 4" gun and 20's on the gun decks. The **TILEFISH** was given to the Venezuelan Navy and renamed the **CARITE** in May 1960.   19N63082

The USS HAMMERHEAD SS364 encrusted with tons of ice during her fresh water cruise in the Great Lakes in November 1943. This boat was built at Manitowoc and was soon to be floated down the Mississippi to salt water. NH70978

SS330	BRILL	"	10/26/44	05/23/48	Turkey 5/48
					Scrapped 78
SS331	BUGARA	"	11/15/44	10/01/70	Floundered 6/71
SS332	BULLHEAD	"	12/04/44		Sunk 08/06/45
SS333	BUMPER	"	12/09/44	11/16/50	Turkey 11/50
SS334	CABEZON	"	12/30/44	05/15/70	Scrapped 12/71
SS335	DENTUDA	"	12/30/44	06/30/67	Scrapped 2/69
SS336	CAPITAINE	"	01/26/45	03/04/66	Italy 3/66
SS337	CARBONERO	"	02/07/45	12/01/70	Target 4/75
SS338	CARP	"	02/28/45	12/20/71	Scrapped 7/73
SS339	CATFISH	"	03/19/45	07/01/71	Argentina 7/71
SS340	ENTEMEDOR	"	04/06/45	07/31/72	Turkey 7/72
SS341	CHIVO	"	04/28/45	07/01/71	Argentina 7/71
SS342	CHOPPER	"	05/25/45	10/01/71	Target 7/76
SS343	CLAMAGORE	"	06/28/45	06/12/45	Museum Charleston, SC
SS344	COBBLER	"	08/08/45	11/21/73	Turkey 11/73
SS345	COCHINO	"	08/25/45		Sunk 8/49
SS346	CORPORAL	"	11/09/45	11/23/73	Turkey 11/73
SS347	CUBERA	"	12/19/45	01/05/72	Venezuela 1/72
SS348	CUSK	"	02/05/46	09/24/69	Scrapped 6/72
SS349	DIODON	"	03/18/46	01/15/71	Scrapped 6/72
SS350	DOGFISH	"	04/29/46	07/28/72	Brazil 7/72
SS351	GREENFISH	"	06/07/46	12/19/73	Brazil 12/73
SS352	HALFBEAK	"	07/22/46	07/01/71	Scrapped 6/72
SS361	GOLET	Man	11/30/43		Sunk 6/44
SS362	GUAVINA	"	12/23/43	06/30/67	Target 11/67
SS363	GUITARRO	"	01/26/44	08/07/54	Turkey 8/54
SS364	HAMMERHEAD	"	03/01/44	10/23/54	Turkey 10/54

A newly added 5"/25 deck gun has been installed on the after deck of the USS SPADEFISH SS411 in this May 1944 photograph. This boat was the first to get the new submarine designed gun. Work started in 1942 on designing the new gun and by mid 1944 it was ready. 19N66132

The **USS BECUNA** SS319 *after commissioning in May 1944. This boat was built at EB and is now a museum ship at Penns Landing in Philadelphia, PA.* USN189867

SS365	HARDHEAD	,,	04/18/44	07/26/72	Greece 7/72	
SS366	HAWKBILL	,,	05/17/44	04/21/53	Netherlands 4/53	
SS367	ICEFISH	,,	06/10/44	02/21/53	Netherlands 2/53	
SS368	JALLAO	,,	07/08/44	06/26/44	Spain 6/74	
SS369	KETE	,,	07/31/44		Sunk 03/20/45	
SS370	KRAKEN	,,	09/08/44	10/24/59	Spain 10/59	
SS371	LAGARTO	,,	10/14/44		Sunk 05/04/45	
SS372	LAMPREY	,,	11/17/44	08/21/60	Argentina 8/60	
SS373	LIZARDFISH	,,	12/30/44	01/09/60	Italy 1/60	
SS374	LOGGERHEAD	,,	02/09/45	06/30/67	Scrapped 8/69	
SS375	MACABI	,,	03/29/45	08/11/60	Turkey 3/60	
SS376	MAPIRO	,,	04/30/45	03/18/60	Turkey 3/60	
SS377	MENHADEN	,,	06/22/45	08/13/71	Target 76	
SS378	MERO	,,	08/17/45	04/20/60	Turkey 4/60	
SS381	SAND LANCE	Ports	10/09/43	09/07/63	Brazil 9/63	
SS382	PICUDA	,,	10/16/43	10/01/72	Spain 10/72	
SS383	PAMPANITO	,,	11/06/43	12/20/71	Museum San Francisco, CA	
SS384	PARCHE	,,	11/20/43	11/08/69	Scrapped 6/70	
SS385	BANG	,,	12/04/43	10/01/72	Spain 10/72	
SS386	PILOTFISH	,,	12/16/43	08/29/46	Bikini Target 10/48	
SS387	PINTADO	,,	01/01/44	03/06/46	Scrapped 2/69	
SS388	PIPEFISH	,,	01/22/44	03/19/46	Scrapped 2/69	
SS389	PIRANHA	,,	02/05/44	05/31/46	Scrapped 8/70	
SS390	PLAICE	,,	02/12/44	09/07/63	Brazil 9/63	
SS391	POMFRET	,,	02/19/44	07/01/71	Turkey 7/71	
SS392	STERLET	,,	03/04/44	09/30/66	Target 1/69	
SS393	QUEENFISH	,,	03/11/44	03/01/63	Target 8/63	
SS394	RAZORBACK	,,	04/03/44	11/30/70	Turkey 11/70	
SS395	REDFISH	,,	04/12/44	06/27/68	Target 2/69	
SS396	RONQUIL	,,	04/22/44	07/01/71	Spain 7/71	
SS397	SCABBARDFISH	,,	04/29/44	02/26/65	Greece 2/65	
SS398	SEGUNDO	,,	05/09/44	08/01/70	Target 8/70	
SS399	SEA CAT	,,	05/16/44	02/12/68	Scrapped 5/73	
SS400	SEA DEVIL	,,	05/24/44	02/17/64	Target 11/64	
SS401	SEA DOG	,,	06/03/44	12/02/68	Scrapped 6/73	
SS402	SEA FOX	,,	06/13/44	12/14/70	Turkey 12/70	
SS403	ATULE	,,	06/21/44	74	Peru 7/74	
SS404	SPIKEFISH	,,	06/30/44	04/02/63	Target 8/64	
SS405	SEA OWL	,,	07/17/44	11/15/69	Scrapped 6/71	
SS406	SEA POACHER	,,	07/31/44	74	Peru 1/74	
SS407	SEA ROBIN	,,	08/07/44	10/01/70	Scrapped 6/71	
SS408	SENNET	,,	08/22/44	12/02/68	Scrapped 6/73	
SS409	PIPER	,,	08/23/44	07/01/70	Scrapped 6/71	
SS410	THREADFIN	,,	08/30/44	08/18/72	Turkey 8/72	
SS411	SPADEFISH	MI	03/09/44	05/03/46	Scrapped 10/69	
SS412	TREPANG	,,	05/22/44	06/30/67	Target 9/69	
SS413	SPOT	,,	08/03/44	01/12/62	Chile 1/62	
SS414	SPRINGER	,,	10/18/44	01/23/61	Chile 1/61	
SS415	STICKLEBACK	,,	03/29/44		Rammed sunk 5/30/58	
SS416	TIRU	,,	10/06/44	05/08/70	Scrapped 9/76	

This overhead view of the **USS BUGARA** SS331 was taken during torpedo practice firings off Panama Bay in January 1945. The torpedo retrieving davits are rigged, which are used for hauling the practice torpedo out of the water. The torpedos float to the surface after their run due to air in the nose of the "fish". Torpedoes with warheads mounted sink if they fail to make contact with a target.

19N76588

The **USS SEALION** SS315 is the only US Submarine to sink a Japanese battleship during World War Two. She sunk the **IJN KONGO** while on her third war patrol, November 21, 1944. The **SEALION** like a few other boats were converted into troop carrying submarines. The torpedo tubes and the engine from the forward engine room were removed to make room for extra living area for 123 troops.

USN233598

The **USS LING** SS297 is wearing a light camouflage paint scheme in this July 1945 photograph. This boat was laid down in November 1942 at Cramp Shipbuilding but due to problems at this yard the boat was completed at the Boston Navy Yard and wasn't commissioned until June 1945. This photograph was taken in July during sea trials. This boat never made it to the Pacific and remained on the east coast. She was decommissioned in 1946 and was used for a reserve training ship from 1960 to 70. She now is a museum in Hackensack, NJ.

19N85741

The "class ship" **USS BALAO SS285** *is seen here at Mare Island during an October 1944 refit. Newly added "SD" tower mast and new lookout platforms are circled along with new TBT's. She still mounts a 4"/50 cal. gun forward.*

19N74361

Another view of the **USS BALAO SS285,** *this time looking aft, shows the addition of a new number one scope and hinges mounted on the stanchions around the guns. These were used to lower the lifeline for a lower angle of fire of the deck guns.*

19N74362

This post-war view of the **USS BLACKFIN SS322** *was taken in June 1946. The boat has just completed a refit at Mare Island and sports all the latest changes and equipment made to the boats near the end of the war and shortly after. Two 5"/25 cal. guns are mounted along with two 40's. The latest antennas and radars are installed and the hull numbers are painted to the side of the fairwater and bow.*

19N95957

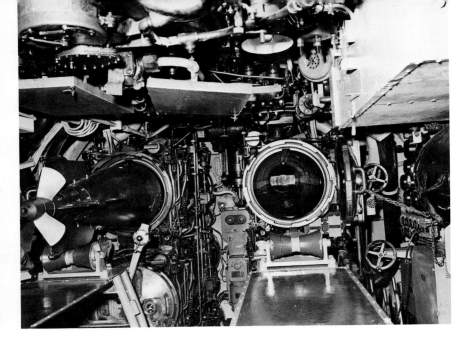

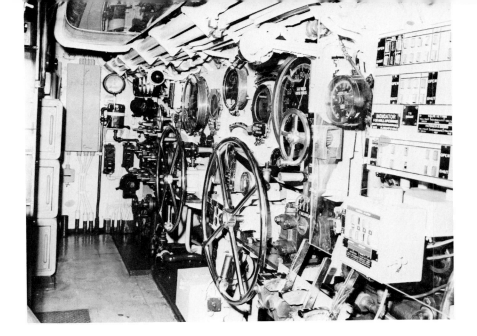

These four photographs are of the interior of the **USS LING SS297**. The top left is looking forward at the torpedo tubes in the forward torpedo room. The door is open on the top right hand tube, while a "fish" is half way loaded into the top left tube. Top right, shows the bow and stern planes control station. The large gauges on the panel are the depth gauges. The panel to the right is the "Christmas tree" which tells which hull openings are shut or open. Bottom left, is looking forward towards the galley in the crew's mess, which is located in the after battery compartment. Twenty-four men can be fed at a sitting. The food is served family style. Bottom right, is a view of the after engine room. In the center is the starboard diesel engine.

Robert F. Sumrall

The **USS CLAMAGORE SS343** is seen here after her "**GUPPY**" refit in July 1948. This conversion produced a sleek looking boat with clean lines. These converted boats served well into the 60's with little topside change. 19N131843

The ex **USS BURRFISH SS312**, is seen here under the flags of Canada. She was turned over to Canada in May 1961 and was recommissioned the **HMCS GRILSE S-71**.   Author

USS TENCH SS417
Jan. 1945

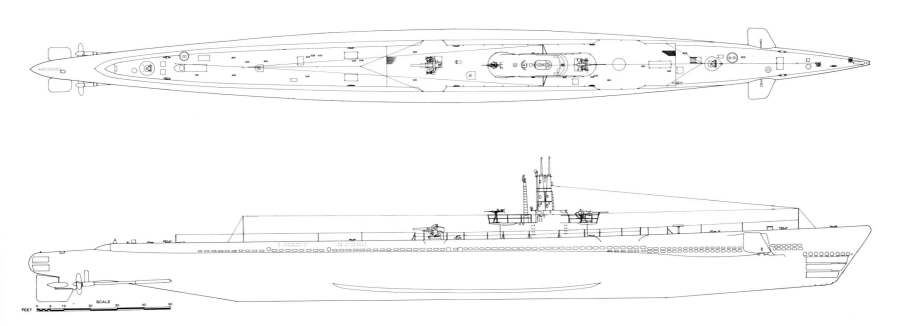

SCALE

FEET 0 5 10   20   30   40   50

*Not too many photographs of **TENCH** class boats were taken during the war for some unknown reason. One of the few is the **USS ARGONAUT SS475**, taken while in the Canal Zone for train-* *ing. This shot was taken in May 1945 before heading on her one and only war patrol. The **TENCH** class like the BALAO's were fitted out with the same topside weapons and radars.* USN

TENCH Class
SS417-437,475-490,522-525
GENERAL INFORMATION

Length Overall	311'-8"
Extreme Beam	27'2"
Standard Displacement	1,570 tons
Submerged Displacement	2,416 tons
Design Complement:	6 Officers 60 Men (1)
Designed Depth:	400 feet
Designed Speed:Surface	20.25 knts
Submerged	8.75 knts
Engines:Diesel	5,400 SHP
Fuel	113,252 gals

(1) Standard crew 85 (WW2)

ARMAMENT
Torpedo Tubes:10
Torpedoes:28
Secondary:1 or 2-40mm single (1945)
     1 or 2-20mm single (1944-45)
     2-.50 cal MG (1944-45)
     2-.30 cal MG (1944-45)

The improved TENCH class was to be the largest class of the fleet boats built, with 145 subs ordered. However, only 31 were completed and the rest were either cancelled in 1944/45 or were scrapped incomplete. The first boat of this new class to be commissioned was the USS TENCH SS417 on 6 October 1944. These boats looked a lot like the BALAOs above the surface, however, their underwater shape near the bow was different. This change was due to the rearrangement of some of the tanks for better hull strength.

These boats incorporated all the latest changes and the latest models of machinery and equipment. Most of the boats were built too late in the war to see much or any war service. These boats, like the others, were modified after the war with snorkel and the superstructure was streamlined. Their performance was so nearly equal to the BALAOs that neither design can be said to have been superior to the other in basic characteristics.

TENCH CLASS

SS417	TENCH	Ports	10/06/44	05/08/70	Peru 1976
SS418	THORNBACK	''	10/13/44	07/01/71	Turkey 71, Scrapped 73
SS419	TIGRONE	''	10/25/44	06/27/75	Target 10/76
SS420	TIRANTE	''	11/06/44	10/01/73	Scrapped 3/74
SS421	TRUTTA	''	11/16/44	07/01/72	Turkey 7/72
SS422	TORO	''	12/08/44	03/11/63	Scrapped 65
SS423	TORSK	''	12/16/44	12/15/71	Museum Baltimore 9/72
SS424	QUILLBACK	''	12/29/44	03/23/73	Scrapped 3/74
SS425	TRUMPETFISH	Cramp	01/29/46	10/15/73	Brazil 10/73
SS426	TUSK	''	04/11/46	10/18/73	Taiwan 10/73
SS427	TURBOT	''			Test hulk
SS428	ULUA	''			Test hulk scrapped 58
SS435	CORSAIR	EB	11/08/46	02/01/63	Scrapped 11/63
SS475	ARGONAUT	Ports	01/15/45	12/02/68	Canada 12/68
SS476	RUNNER	''	02/06/45	12/15/71	Scrapped 6/73
SS477	CONGER	''	02/14/45	07/23/63	Scrapped 7/64
SS478	CUTLASS	''	03/17/45	04/12/73	Taiwan 4/73
SS479	DIABLO	''	03/31/45	06/01/64	Pakistan 6/64
SS480	MEDREGEL	''	04/14/45	08/01/70	Scrapped 6/72
SS481	REQUIN	''	04/28/45	12/20/71	Museum Tampa 7/72
SS482	IREX	''	05/14/45	11/17/69	Scrapped 9/71
SS483	SEA LEOPARD	''	06/11/45	03/27/73	Brazil 3/73
SS484	ODAX	''	07/11/45	07/08/72	Brazil 7/72
SS486	POMODON	''	09/11/45	08/01/70	Scrapped 1/72
SS487	REMORA	''	01/03/46	10/29/73	Greece 10/73
SS488	SARDA	''	04/19/46	06/01/64	Scrapped 5/65
SS489	SPINAX	''	09/20/46	01/11/69	Scrapped 6/72
SS490	VOLADOR	''	10/01/48	08/18/72	Italy 8/72
SS522	AMBERJACK	Bos	03/04/46	10/17/73	Brazil 10/73
SS523	GRAMPUS	''	10/26/49	05/13/72	Brazil 5/72
SS524	PICKEREL	Ports	04/04/49	08/18/72	Italy 8/72
SS525	GRENADIER	Bos	02/10/51	05/15/73	Venezuela 5/73

*The **USS SARDA SS488** is seen here shortly after the war. She still retains her war time configuration except for a few new sonar domes located on her deck forward and fixed life lines topside.*

USN442627

*Another postwar view of a **TENCH** class boat, this time the **USS TORO SS422**. All deck guns have been removed and a few new pieces of electronic gear.*

USN

U. S. SUBMARINE WALRUS
DOWN THE WAYS
SEPTEMBER 20, 1946
ELECTRIC BOAT CO. GROTON, CONN.

*The incomplete **USS WALRUS SS437** slides down the ways at the Electric Boat Co., on September 20, 1946. This boat was laid down in June 1945 and with the end of the war construction was suspended. The hull was finally scrapped in 1958.*   19N96508

*The **USS PICKEREL SS 524** was modified into the **GUPPY** configuration and is seen here in April 1955, off Hawaii. The scopes are extended and have protective sleeves that are camouflaged.*

USN681431

This photo of the shears of the **USS REMORA SS486** was taken February 7, 1946. This looks very much like a late wartime boat. A latest model of the "SJ" radar is installed along with a base for a whip antenna mounted to the "SV" mast housing. Mounted to the left of the life ring is a flare pot and to the right is a mounting for a machine gun. Note the camouflage paint applied to the face of the bridge and number one scope housing.

19N92667

41

Like the other boats that saw postwar service, modifications were made. Here the **USS POMODON SS486** is seen with the early GUPPY ''sail''. The wood decks have been replaced with metal, in fact the entire superstructure is new. This photograph was taken on 27 June 1947 at Mare Island Naval Shipyard.

19N129308

This 1950's photograph of the **USS POMODON SS486** is a typical **"GUPPY"** conversion. These boats saw many years of service and some lasted into the 1970's. The dome mounted on the port side is for sonar.

USN

Like most ships after the war, they were laid up in reserve and never saw service again. Here at the Pacific Reserve Fleet, Mare Island, ships and submarines set at berths 53, 54, 55, and 56. This photograph was taken on July 12, 1960.

NH88080

43

Near the end of their service, these "guppy" fleet boats only have a few months and years left. This photograph was taken at New London, in the late 1960's. From left to right are, unknown, USS SEA ROBIN SS407, USS TUSK SS426, USS SEA OWL SS405, USS SABLEFISH SS303, USS HALFBEAK SS352, USS BLENNY SS324, USS BECUNA SS319.

The USS SNOOK SS279 is seen here in this January 11, 1943 photograph taken off Portsmouth, NH. Her number two scope is shown fully raised and the boat is equipped with two 20mm guns on her gun decks. This boat was lost in April 1945.

FLEET SUBMARINES LOST OR SEVERELY DAMAGED DURING WW2

USS GROWLER SS215 was sunk by Japanese ASW forces west of the Philippines on 8 November 1944. This was the veteran sub's 11th war patrol. She was lost while attacking a convoy with pack mates HAKE and HARDHEAD. All hands were lost with the boat on her first war patrol.

USS GRUNION SS216 was probably lost on 30 July 1942 off Kiska, by unknown causes. She was lost with all hands.

USS ALBACORE SS218 was lost by hitting a mine on 7 November 1944 off northern Japan. This was her 11th war patrol and she was lost with all hands.

USS AMBERJACK SS219 while on her third war patrol, was attacked and sunk by Japanese ASW forces on 16 February 1943. She was sunk with all hands.

USS BONEFISH SS223 was sunk by enemy action on 18 June 1945 off the west coast of Japan. This was her 8th war patrol and she was lost with all hands.

USS CORVINA SS226 was the only US sub sunk by torpedo fire from an enemy submarine. While on her maiden patrol, she was hit by two torpedos fired by I-176 on 16 November 1943 off Truk. She was lost with all 82 of her crew.

USS DARTER SS227 was lost on her 4th war patrol by running aground off Bombay Shoal, Philippines 24 October 1944. Her crew were rescued by the DACE.

USS HERRING SS233 was sunk by shore batteries off Kurile Islands on 1 June 1944. This was her 8th war patrol and she was lost with all hands.

USS TRIGGER SS237 while on her 12th war patrol was attacked by enemy forces on 28 March 1945. She was lost with all hands.

USS WAHOO SS238 was sunk by depth charges from Japanese aircraft while on her 6th war patrol off the coast of Japan. She was lost with all hands.

USS DORADO SS248 was sunk enroute to the Panama Canal by US aircraft on 12 October 1943. She was lost with all hands.

USS FLIER SS250 was sunk by hitting a mine while on the surface as she transitted the Balabac Strait on 13 August 1944. She was just starting her 2nd war patrol. Eight men survived and were picked up by the **USS REDFIN SS272**.

USS HARDER SS257 was lost on her 6th war patrol by depth charging by Japanese ASW craft off the Philippines. She was lost with all hands on 24 August 1944.

USS ROBALO SS273 was sunk by a mine off the Philippines on 26 July 1944, while on her 3rd war patrol. Four men survived the sinking but were captured by the Japanese and taken prisoner.

USS RUNNER SS275 failed to return from her 2nd war patrol off the coast of Japan in June 1943.

USS SCAMP SS277 was lost while on her 8th war patrol off Tokyo Bay by depth charge on 11 November 1944. She was lost with all hands.

USS SCORPION SS278 was lost in the Yellow Sea by hitting a mine on 5 January 1944. She was on her 4th war patrol and was lost with all hands.

USS SNOOK SS279 was lost in the Luzon Straits on 8 April 1945 while on her 8th war patrol. She was lost with all hands.

USS TULLIBEE SS284 was sunk by her own torpedo on 26 March 1944 off Pelew Island. This was her 4th war patrol. Only one man survived.

USS CAPELIN SS289 was missing with all hands while on her 2nd war patrol off Celebes December 1943.

USS CISCO SS290 was sunk on her first war patrol by Japanese aircraft on Mindanao, 28 September 1943. She was lost with all hands.

USS ESCOLAR SS294 was lost on her 1st war patrol in the Yellow Sea in October 1944. The cause of loss is unknown. She was lost with all hands.

USS LANCETFISH SS296 sank at the pier in Boston Navy Yard during completion on 15 March 1945. She was raised but de-commissioned incomplete.

USS TANG SS306 was sunk by her own torpedo that made a circular run on 24 October 1944 off Formosa. This was her 5th war patrol and nine men survived the sinking.

USS SHARK SS314 was lost during her 3rd war patrol off Luzon. She was attacked by Japanese ASW forces 24 October 1944. All hands were lost with the boat.

USS BARBEL SS316, while on her 4th war patrol, was bombed by Japanese aircraft and sunk 4 February 1945 with all hands off Palawan.

USS BULLHEAD SS332 was sunk by Japanese aircraft off Bali 6 August 1945 with all hands while on her 3rd patrol.

USS GOLET SS361 was missing while on her 2nd war patrol. She was probably sunk by Japanese ASW forces 14 June 1944 with all hands.

USS KETE SS369 was missing after 20 March 1945 while on her 2nd war patrol with all hands.

USS LAGARTO SS371 was sunk by a Japanese minelayer in the Gulf of Siam 4 May 1945. This was her maiden war patrol and she was lost with all hands.

The largest sub built for the US Navy are the Trident Missile Submarines over 560 feet long. These nuclear powered ballistic missile boats carry 24 tubes which can fire the Trident missile to a range of over 6,000 miles. These boats carry a crew of 160 and can stay on patrol as long as the food lasts.

USN

POSTWAR SUBMARINES

In the postwar years, some of the World War Two submarines were used as active Fleet units. Most of the boats to serve after the war had their exteriors changed with the introduction of snorkel. The boats went through a modernization program called "GUPPY" which streamlined the superstructure and removed most of the guns. These boats served into the late 60s and early 70s, but were replaced by the build-up of the nuclear submarine.

Other boats were converted into Radar Picket and troop transport submarines. These troop subs retained the appearance of WW2 boats with the open shears and deck guns. Some boats were modified to carry the early surface launched rockets, which lead up to the nuclear missile submarine of today. More than a half dozen boats have been saved as museums through the country and are in various stages of configurations.

During the postwar years, approximately seventy-six boats were transferred to fourteen friendly foreign navies. Most of these boats served more time in those navies than they did in the US Navy.

Several classes of submarines have been built since the war and since the early 60s, two basic types of submarines are used in the US Navy, the attack submarine and the missile submarine. The STURGEON class built between 1967-75 with 37 units and the new LOS ANGELES class with over 60 boats built or laid down to date are the mainstay of the Navy's attack submarine fleet. Both of these classes are nuclear propelled. The first true missile submarines were the GEORGE WASHINGTON class, built 1959-67. They were 425 feet long and were equipped with 16 missile tubes, which fired a missile from the top of the after superstructure. The newest class of missile boat being built is the OHIO class. This boat is 560 feet long and fires the new Trident missile. It carries 24 of them. Plans call for 20 of these boats to be built. There are about 8 in service now. These boats are the largest boats built and you could put a WW2 Fleet boat inside.

Here the **USS MEMPHIS SSN691** on sea trials churns up the sea. These boats unlike the WW2 fleet boats were designed for submerged running. Note that the bridge has only enough room for about three crewmembers. These boats are the mainstay of the attack submarine force.   USN

With the missile age upon us in the late 50's the US Navy started to design boats that would carry a number of missiles. These were carried in pressure proof containers which could be fired submerged. Here the first of these ballistic missile submarines (SSBN) the **USS GEORGE WASHINGTON SSBN598** is being completed at the Electric Boat Company in November 1959. These boats were nuclear powered and would go on a submerged patrol for 60 or more days straight.   USN